How t

Boys:

Secrets of Raising Healthy Sons and Helping Them to Become Mature, Clever, Strong and Happy Men

By

Eva Delano

Table of Contents

How to Raise Boys: Secrets of Raising Healthy Sons and Helping Them to Become Mature, Clever, Strong and Happy Men

By Eva Delano

First Published, 2015

Printed in the United States of America

Introduction

Parents always want what is best for their children. However, raising boys can be a daunting and exhausting task. This is because unlike girls, boys are more likely to drop out of school, indulge in drug abuse, commit suicide, become part of crime gangs and commit numerous other vices. These probabilities are worrying and serve to remind parents that the boy child is highly vulnerable. Perhaps this is why most parents will agree that raising boys in the right way to help them mature and become strong, clever and happy men is more demanding.

Every time a mother holds her newborn baby in her arms, she knows that everything she does from that moment on counts. Her actions and of those around her directly influence her child and to some extent they directly dictate the kind of lifestyle—including life decisions—that her child will make. However, this should not scare you as a parent. There are some basic principles which when applied correctly may help you to successfully raise your son into a decent man with morals. Outlined below are the role of mother and father in parenting and in encouragement, the importance of sports and winning, mastering emotions and how to help a son find his passion and path in life.

Chapter 1. Basic Principles on How to Raise Boys The Right Way

Be affectionate towards him

As children, boys love it when you give them frequent hugs and kisses throughout the day and before retiring to bed. At this stage they tend to be closer to their parents (especially their mothers). Soon as they hit adolescent stage, things change. They gain the sense of independence and they may tend to break away from their parents (especially their mothers). They may even stop appreciating the frequent hugs and kisses like they used to. This does not mean that you should stop giving them.

Establish good timing. For example, it would be better to give him just a peck on the way to bed or occasionally in the morning before breakfast or before he heads to school. He is more likely to feel embarrassed if you kiss him before his friends. Whenever he is feeling down, give him a brief hug to show him that you care. Always remember that boys always long for the caring touch of a mother even if they act like they don't. Men give out affection because they grew up getting it. This means that affectionate men experienced physical tenderness when they were younger.

Show him how to respect others

This can be done by creating an environment where he will grow up obeying rules, listening to people in authority and interacting in a caring way. This will act as the baseline for showing respect to everyone around him. As a result, he will grow up to become a man of honor.

You can do this by setting rules and consequences. Boys respect people who keep them alert and conscious of their decisions. If he breaks a rule- whether breaking a curfew, using abusive or unacceptable language, or being rude- let him know the consequences and enforce them. Failure to do this will make him lose motivation and over time, he might become rude and less caring.

Be a good role model to your son. Respect every adult in your son's life (for example his teachers, coaches and all the others). If there is a conflict – let's say between him and his coach- handle the situation gracefully. Do not rush into taking sides with your son. First, listen to both sides of the story before making your conclusion. If you find out that your son is right, explain to him that it is still not acceptable to be rude to his coach. Promise him that you will speak to his coach to see how you can resolve the situation. Then remind him that if any other conflict ever arises again with his coach, he should let you know instead of talking back to his coach. By doing this, your will have taught your son important problem-solving skills and at the same time emphasized on the importance of showing respect.

Strengthen his self-esteem

Men who feel good about themselves are sometimes labeled as being egotistical. However, this is not always the case. When a man feels good about himself, it means that he has confidence, competence and that he is feeling worthy. Isn't this exactly what you want for your son?

Stop giving him false praise and be specific. For example, instead of saying that he is the smartest kid in the world, try praising his efforts rather than his talents. Congratulate him for getting the work done

9

and appreciate his hard work rather than giving him general complements.

Be very careful about the messages you give your kid as he is growing up. Never use his gender to justify his mistakes; doing this will make him grow up believing that he has no control over his actions just because he is a boy. Therefore he will start believing that boys are troublemakers and he will grow up to be one himself.

Teach him how to empathize

When a boy is able to understand the feelings of others, it makes him a better friend. This will be transformed into becoming a better husband and a better father in the future. Empathy is a valuable skill in your son's social life. It is a valuable foundation in your son's life but one of the most difficult traits to instill due to the violent environment we are living in. Teach your son how to put himself in other people's situations.

Encourage him to try and understand other people's feelings. You can do this by using examples from things which he enjoys doing like sports. For example, if he likes watching football, you could join him on the couch. Fabricate some questions from the situation of the game and see how he responds to them. This will teach him to always consider other people's feelings.

Encourage him to develop a reading culture especially fiction materials. This is because the part of the brain that enables us to understand and interpret the feelings of the characters in the fictional stories is the same one that enables us to understand and interpret the feelings of people in real life. This means that if he becomes fond of reading fictional books, he will develop some empathy towards people and he will have a stronger ability to understand those around him.

Chapter 2. Role of Mother and Father in Parenting and in Encouragement

The father always has one advantage over the mother when it comes to raising boys. This is because he knows the point of view of his son due to his gender. A mother can help in encouraging his son to be a good man but a father actually shows him how to do it. This can be done in the ways discussed below:

As a father, make sure that you will always be there for your son when he most needs you. A father figure and a husband figure are known to provide a sense of security for the family. A son needs to know and feel like the dad enjoys spending time with him. This simple move means a lot to a son. He will interpret it as his father loves him, he enjoys his company and that he can always count on his dad. He will know that his dad is good and as a result he will always look up to his father as a good role model. In the end he will grow up to become a good dad himself.

Always treat women with respect. The only way a son learns how to relate with women is by watching his father. Therefore, when a dad is interacting with women, he should do so in a respective way, this includes saying sorry when he is wrong (admitting his mistakes), speaking and conducting himself with respect at all times. A dad should also be in a position to handle arguments in a reasonable way especially when arguing with his wife. The son is always watching and high chance is that he will follow his father's footsteps closely.

Engage in physical activity with your son. As a dad, try to involve your son in some physical activities such as playful wrestling and roughhousing. This will teach your son how to regulate his emotions. It will also aid them on how to control their physical impulses. In addition, boys always find the physical touch of a father to be quite reassuring and they also appreciate kisses and hugs from their dad.

As a mother, your role is mostly in providing emotional support. Encourage him throughout his achievements and correct him where he goes wrong. Instill respect in him and teach him good problem-solving skills. Teach him how to empathize with others.

Both parents should work together in ensuring that their son's needs are well taken care of. They should draw a good image for the son as parents; meaning that they should show unity, love, care and affection in the family.

Both parents should follow up in the child's academic performance. If he is not performing as expected they should encourage him to work harder in school and if necessary they should hire a private tutor to help him improve his performance. They should encourage their son to go out and play with other kids. This will help him in building a strong social network.

When young, boys generally like playing with tools and objects. Parents should ensure that at least their son has some toys to play with, like toy cars. Boys naturally like to fix things and this should be taken into consideration by ensuring that there is enough room in the house to play. Parents should also ensure that sharp objects and other potentially harmful materials or even things that could easily get damaged are placed at a safe distance from the child.

It is also important for the parents to set aside some time just for the family to spend time together. This will provide a platform for them to study the progress of their son and take note of any changes in their behavior which could be a warning sign that he is heading the wrong direction. Setting aside some family time will also teach your son the importance of establishing strong kinship ties. As a result, he will pass over these values to his family in future.

Another important point on having family time is that, one of the parents can see something in the boy which the other parent had not seen. This is because women interpret things in a different way as compared to men. For example, when a boy suddenly becomes an introvert, one may interpret it that he is just taking some time off his schedule while the other may see that maybe he is undergoing emotional stress. This will help both parents learn more about their son and look for ways to help him out.

The dad can sometimes include his son to some of his outings like when he is going to watch a football or baseball match or when he is going for training or just to the gym to work out. These outdoor activities can help him identify his son's talents. It will also establish a stronger bond between them and the son will know that he always has a shoulder to lean on.

Spending time with the dad will also help the boy in making rational decisions and handle situations in a mature way. Boys who grow up with a strong social support are more likely to accomplish their goals and become successful as compared to their counterparts who lack support. A strong social network also makes life a little bit easier for the boy. This will translate into him living a happier life.

Parents can start encouraging their son from his younger age. This can be done by rewarding every good deed he does. This will increase his motivation and he will grow up challenging his abilities more and more and thus each and every day he will work towards becoming a better person. In future, he will return the favor by helping and encouraging those around him to become successful.

Parents should also teach their son to become financially independent since naturally boys are known to be the providers in the family. Guide him on how to manage his finances and how to make investments wisely. They should also teach him how to deal with his mistakes in a mature way. This will prevent him from repeating the same mistakes in future.

Chapter 3. Mastering Emotions

Some traits such as the macho tough guy and the strong silent type have been portrayed to be the most appealing on big screens. However, this may not be the case in real life since the good guys should know how to deal with their emotions in the right way. The society at large has portrayed some qualities as 'manly', but in real sense they are repressive. It dictates that men should be in control and stoic; that they should never show how they feel.

In most cases, a girl's emotions are taken care of better than a boy's emotions. Most times a girl will be asked how she feels while for a boy it happens only once a while. When a girl gets hurt, she will be comforted while a boy might be told to 'be a man, it's not that bad'. Once this is done, a boy will start learning how to hide his feelings. As a result, he will grow up to be a man who cannot communicate his emotions. He will be bottling them up or lashing out and this will largely affect his relationship with others. To prevent this situation, there are some ways you can use to get him to open up to you.

Let him know you are there for him

If you notice that your son looks grumpy and withdrawn after school, don't flock him with questions, just offer to hear him out. Tell him that you have noticed that he is upset and let him know you are there to help if you can. Bring up the topic later on in a conversation. Tell him that you are concerned that something bad might have happened at school. This will create a good rapport between you two and he might let you in (Math is boring). Echo his feelings (yeah, Math can be boring sometimes).

High chance he will open up: That teacher gives me many difficult sums. This would be a good moment to validate his feelings and weigh out his options, but coax out: You do get many difficult sums. What sums did you get today? The kid will be confident that you are on his side and so he will give you more information in depth knowing that you are not going to give him a lecture.

You should help him find a solution

Getting your son to open up is one thing while getting him to understand that bad feelings may thrive but they do not last is another. When dealing with boys it is important to focus on the problem rather than the emotion involved. Part of parenting involves teaching your son that emotions- whether fear, anger, pain or sadness – may linger and that it is ok. After some time he will begin to feel better.

For example, if your son fails to make it into the most popular football team, he will be greatly disappointed. Just give him time to cool down then let him pour his heart out. Then let him know that it is not the end for him. Give him other options and let him know that he could start out small and build up to where he wants to go and in the end he can still achieve his goals.

When your son learns to master his emotions, he will live a happier and more fulfilling life. This is because bottling up emotions may lead to problems in anger management and as a result he might become violent towards those around him.

It is also important for him to speak out his mind so that he may be corrected where he is wrong. This will prevent him from making mistakes in the future which could have been easily prevented if he had spoken out in good time.

Mastering emotions can also prevent him from acquiring some lifestyle diseases such as stomach ulcers and hypertension which result from stress. So by doing this you are also taking care of your son's future health. This will also build his character into an outgoing and very active young man. Most women find men with these traits to be more attractive than their less active counterparts.

Chapter 4. Importance of Sports and Winning

Sports are very important in a kid's life. This is because it helps him build a healthy mind, a healthy body, important life skills and friendships. By starting out from a younger age, your son will grow up to be part of the game. This is important since it will aid your son to go through the emotional rollercoaster in an appropriate, safe and well structured environment.

Sport teaches your son how to be part of a team, how to bounce back from a major loss, how to win well and how to go through unpleasant scenarios such as injuries. Sport teaches your child to set goals and challenges for himself and as a result he will always be aiming higher and trying harder even if it doesn't mean he has to win.

A good thing about sport is that the only thing that counts is your son's effort. For example, your son might have spent the whole day running around and kicking the ball. Even if their team doesn't win, what matters most is that your son did his best because the only thing that he had in control was his effort.

As parents it is important that you encourage a sporting attitude both at home, on the sideline and as your child gets older. Boys always like pleasing their parents and making the proud. Parents can take advantage of this and use it to encourage a sporting attitude at home. For example, when watching a game at home, beware of the comments you make. Cheer up your team's efforts even if they are on the losing end. Avoid using abusive language or jeering as this will send a negative message to your son about the game.

It is also a good idea to give your son some examples of athletes who don't always win but they are known to be talented. This will pass on the message that a game is not always about winning but about the efforts that each one puts in as a team. When your son gets home from a sporting event, don't rush into asking about who won or lost the game. Ask him if he had a good time and if he enjoyed himself first. By doing this, you will be able to understand what your boy is aiming to gain from the sport.

On the sideline, be very careful on the comments you make when you attend a sporting event with your son. If your team is not winning, it is better to wish them better luck next time than wondering how they could miss that shot. Encourage them to keep going, they are almost there instead of wondering if they could run any faster.

Let your body language and your tone in check when addressing your son. Don't make him feel like you are angry with him just because he missed a shot. This will make him lose interest in the sport because he will feel like he is not good enough. Your son is always looking up to you, so if you show him that you are having fun and you sound positive then he will reflect the same.

As your son gets older, the strategies change and this time encourage them to focus on winning. However, this might leave out some boys. Some boys may lose interest in the sport. You can still involve them by encouraging them to join new teams or find out other fun activities to keep them occupied but still reap the same benefits from the sport.

When your son does not want to play sport anymore, try to find out his reasons. If they can be easily overcome help him get through it, if not then help him find other options. If he just doesn't want to start doing competitive games, there are still other fun activities like dancing, cycling, skateboarding, rollerblading, flying kites, beach activities and so many options to choose from.

Chapter 5. How to Help Your Son to Find His Passion and Path in Life

As parents, it is important to know that you should not enforce or make decisions on behalf of your son. Your role is to guide him and encourage him throughout his journey. Some kids seemingly come out of the womb knowing what their passion is, others just inherit talents from their parents grow up perfecting their skills. For example, a kid who grows up in a circus may be talented in doing many amazing things like learning the art of magic or he may be good at making unimaginable contortions with his body. If he grows up near a gymnasium, he might develop interest in gymnastics and grow up to become quite good at it.

However, it is not guaranteed that your son's environment fully dictates his passion and path in life. As a parent, it is important to get involved in your son's lifestyle. Try to establish if he is more of an introvert, an extrovert or an ambivert. What are his hobbies? What is he exceptionally good at? These are some of the questions that you can use to guide him towards finding his passion. For example, he might be good at drawing when it comes to singing, no one sings better than him. Find out what is unique about him and build on that. For instance in the above example, you can encourage him to join the school choir or enroll him in a school of arts in order to build on his abilities.

Be with him throughout the journey and let him know that he can always count on you for support. If possible, attend all the important events where he is performing. If he tries out a particular path and things don't work out as he had expected, encourage him and give him other options. Sometimes the best option might be to quit! This is because sometimes a kid may believe that he knows what is best for him yet it is so obvious that he is not cut out for that. In such an instance, when the time comes, there is no shame in losing or quitting. However, this should be used as the last option. Don't rush into telling him to quit every time he loses a game. Give him time for himself. Don't make him feel as if he is under pressure to perform. Give him room to make mistakes and learn from them.

Conclusion

After all is said and done, it is important to understand that there is no cut out manual about parenting that works out for every kid since every child is different and unique in his own way and what works on your son may not work out on another parent's kids. However, there are some basic principles which when followed may make parenting to be an easier task.

Some of them have been outlined above and we hope that this will help you learn how to raise boys the right way. Wishing you all the best!

Thank You Page

I want to personally thank you for reading my book. I hope you found information in this book useful and I would be very grateful if you could leave your honest review about this book. I certainly want to thank you in advance for doing this.

If you have the time, you can check my other books too.

Lightning Source UK Ltd.
Milton Keynes UK
UKHW02f2318060118
315630UK00014B/704/P